DISCOVER YOUR
Gifts
WORKBOOK

TWELVE SESSIONS FOR EXPLORING
YOUR GOD-GIVEN PURPOSE

TONY COOK AND DON EVERTS

EVERY GIFT

Everyone's a gift with gifts to share

ENTREPRENEURIAL · MANAGEMENT · FINANCIAL · CRITICAL THINKING · ARTISTIC · CIVIC · VOTE · INTERCULTURAL · COMMUNICATION · LEADERSHIP · TEAMWORK · TECHNICAL · INTERPERSONAL

An imprint of InterVarsity Press
Downers Grove, Illinois

InterVarsity Press
P.O. Box 1400, Downers Grove, IL 60515-1426
ivpress.com
email@ivpress.com

InterVarsity Press® is the book-publishing division of InterVarsity Christian Fellowship/USA®, a movement of students and faculty active on campus at hundreds of universities, colleges, and schools of nursing in the United States of America, and a member movement of the International Fellowship of Evangelical Students. For information about local and regional activities, visit intervarsity.org.

Scripture quotations, unless otherwise noted, are from The Holy Bible, English Standard Version, copyright © 2001 by Crossway Bibles, a division of Good News Publishers. Used by permission. All rights reserved.

While any stories in this book are true, some names and identifying information may have been changed to protect the privacy of individuals.

All figures unless otherwise noted are designed by Sarah Eischer; Gift icons by OX Creative, copyright Lutheran Hour Ministries.

The publisher cannot verify the accuracy or functionality of website URLs used in this book beyond the date of publication.

Cover design and image composite: David Fassett
Interior design: Jeanna Wiggins
Images: light blue abstract: © andipantz / iStock / Getty Images Plus
      fine grain pattern: © GOLDsquirrel / iStock / Getty Images Plus
      cardboard texture: © Katsumi Murouchi / Moment / Getty Images
      flame illustration: © Pobytov / DigitalVision Vectors / Getty Images
      abstract pattern: © Wako Megumi / iStock / Getty Images Plus
      silhouettes of teens: © wundervisuals / E+ / Getty Images
      acrylic abstract: © Wylius / iStock / Getty Images Plus

ISBN 978-1-5140-0449-4 (print)
ISBN 978-1-5140-0450-0 (digital)

Printed in the United States of America ♾

InterVarsity Press is committed to ecological stewardship and to the conservation of natural resources in all our operations. This book was printed using sustainably sourced paper.

P	20	19	18	17	16	15	14	13	12	11	10	9	8	7	6	5	4	3	2	1
Y	39	38	37	36	35	34	33	32	31	30	29	28	27	26	25	24	23	22		

DEDICATED

to the countless people who

use their gifts to the glory of God

and the love of their neighbor

Contents

Everyone Is a Gift with Gifts to Share

W e believe that you are a gift with gifts to share and that God has entrusted these gifts to you to help you be a blessing in every area of your life. And here's the thing: we believe the same is true about every person you've ever met or will meet. We are all gifts with gifts to share.

That's why we've created this workbook: to encourage more and more people to discover their God-given gifts, share those gifts generously with the world, and grow those gifts over time.

A BIBLICAL VIEW OF HUMANS

The Bible is very clear that God is the Creator of all humans and, whether we acknowledge him or not, we are all created by him (Genesis 1:31). Even after our horrid fall from the Garden, the Bible affirms that we are each "fearfully and wonderfully made" (Psalm 139:14). We are all gifts.

And we are all gifted. The Bible is clear right from the beginning that God created humans to do good, flourishing work on the earth and that he blessed them with the gifts and resources they would need to do that work (Genesis 1:28).

While Christians typically focus on spiritual gifts needed for the work of ministry (1 Corinthians 12), all humans are blessed with natural or common gifts needed for the work we have been put on earth to pursue. These natural gifts (including our aptitudes, innate abilities, and acquired skills) are also entrusted to us by God. As James put it, "Every good gift and every perfect gift is from above, coming down from the Father of lights" (James 1:17).

DISCOVERING YOUR GIFTS

While Christians use many resources designed to help them discover their spiritual gifts, they don't as often explore the natural gifts God has entrusted to them and all humans. As a result, many of these aptitudes, abilities, and skills go unused or underused over time.

This is why we developed the EveryGift Inventory, a research-based approach to helping people discern what natural gifts God has given them in twelve distinct areas. In the following pages, we will introduce you to all twelve gifts and provide prompts and exercises to help you not only discover more of your own God-given gifts, but those of the people around you as well. Because we are focusing on natural gifts, this workbook can be used by people of any faith or no faith at all. Discovering gifts is an important first step. From there, you can put thought into how you can generously share those gifts in various areas of life and how you can grow those gifts over time.

SHARING YOUR GIFTS

God not only gives us gifts but also calls us to certain work. We live out our purpose on earth most effectively when we are faithful to our specific, God-given callings, or *vocations*. As Paul put it, "Let each person lead the life that the Lord has assigned to him, and to which God has called him" (1 Corinthians 7:17).

Our vocations are the different roles and relationships God calls us to in life. While many associate *calling* with missionary or church work, the biblical doctrine of vocation also includes the "ordinary tasks and roles of human life" that God calls all of us to in our households, our local churches, our work, and our communities.[1]

This workbook provides prompts and exercises to help you explore how you could be sharing each of the gifts you discover in your specific vocations in every area of your life.

GROWING YOUR GIFTS

Once you've discovered and started to share your gifts, there's one more step: consider how to sharpen, develop, and grow those gifts more over time. As Paul Stanley and Robert Clinton put it, "We all have

a stewardship responsibility to continue to develop what God has given us."[2] When it comes to the good, flourishing work God has given us to do on earth, we don't want to just get it done—we want to do it well.

We can help each other become faithful stewards as we develop our gifts. Paul invited Christians to do this when he wrote, "Therefore encourage one another and build one another up, just as you are doing" (1 Thessalonians 5:11).

As you think about ways you or others can grow your gifts, consider three different aspects of growth: knowledge, attitude, and skills. *Knowledge* in a gift area is important to develop—even if you are a "natural," you can grow your gift by increasing your knowledge through reading, classes, video training, being mentored, and so on. *Attitude* about a gift area can also be nurtured over time—your beliefs, opinions, and feelings are directly linked with your motivation, so you can grow your attitude through reflection, conversation, celebration, gratitude, and even prayer. Finally, you can always work on specific *skills* through practice, mentoring, repetition, and coaching.

UNLEASHING EVERY GIFT

The two of us (Tony Cook and Don Everts) have come to this topic of unleashing people's gifts with conviction and passion. As a pastor and professor, Tony has seen firsthand the detrimental effects that come from people seeing themselves or others as less than gifts. As a result, Tony has spent considerable time and energy conducting nationwide research related to this topic. You can read more about the findings in the research monograph *Gifted for More: A New Framework for Equipping Christians to Share Their Abilities and Skills in Everyday Life.*[3]

As a campus missionary and pastor, Don has witnessed the power of people who are inspired and equipped to use the gifts God has given them. So Don has delved deep into the biblical material that relates to our gifts. You can read more about this biblical anthropology and related stories from church history and everyday life in *Discover Your Gifts: Celebrating How God Made You and Everyone You Know.*[4]

This workbook is a companion to these other books and is designed to help you discover more of your gifts, share those gifts generously with the world, and grow those gifts over time. To get the most out of this workbook, we invite you to first take the EveryGift Inventory.

The EveryGift Inventory will help you discover the aptitudes, innate abilities, and acquired skills that make up your unique gifts in twelve distinct areas. The inventory will take less than twenty minutes to complete and will provide you a personalized (absolutely free) overview of your gifts. Go to www.everygift.org to get started. Once you have your personalized results, you can work through this material in a couple of ways.

Option 1: Flip to the chapters that cover the specific gifts called out in your personalized EveryGift results. The advantage to this approach is that it helps you focus right away on your own gifts.

Option 2: Work through each chapter sequentially. Because our exercises are designed to help you think through not only your own gifts but also those of people around you, this approach will better allow you to discover gifts in others and consider how you can help them unleash their gifts.

Whether you are working through this workbook alone, with a small group, or as part of a class, this is the ultimate goal: the unleashing of gifts.

God has given us gifts so that we will use them with purpose in the places he calls us to be. The more we discover, share, and grow our gifts, the more we are unleashing our God-given gifts for the good, flourishing work God has assigned to us. So our final encouragement as you dive into the following pages is the same that Paul had for the Christians living in Rome:

"Having gifts that differ according to the grace given to us, let us use them" (Romans 12:6).

May we all use the gifts God has given us.

SESSION ONE
Technical Gifts

*You shall speak to all the skillful, whom I have filled
with a spirit of skill, that they make Aaron's garments.*

EXODUS 28:3

*You've got to learn your instrument. Then, you practice,
practice, practice. And then, when you finally get up
there on the bandstand, forget all that and just wail.*

CHARLIE PARKER, AMERICAN SAXOPHONIST

Professionally, Tony is a leader, researcher, pastor, and educator—
and he uses a variety of the gifts entrusted to him in his work. But
over the years Tony has also developed a surprising technical gift that
has little to do with his day job.

There is a wide variety of technical gifts, of course. In our nationwide
research we asked people if they had any gifts that helped them perform
specific tasks that required a special and refined set of skills. These are
what we call technical gifts, and respondents listed a wide variety of
skills: baking, photography, sewing, cooking, problem identification,
planning events, exegeting Scripture, computer knowledge, fixing, language acquisition, health care, real estate, electronic and optical materials, teaching math (including engineering calculus), computer repair,
gardening, painting and general house repair, music, media production,
organizing and scheduling, and more.[1]

When Tony took the survey, he listed "digitally mixing music" as one
of his technical gifts! But what does digitally mixing music have in
common with baking, gardening, and general house repair? They all
have this in common: *technical gifts help you perform specific tasks that
require a special and refined set of skills.*

All technical skills can be used to promote the common good. Additionally, they can be further developed over time with practice. While many people have technical gifts, there are some people for whom these gifts are a significant part of their lives. In a national survey, 8 percent of respondents listed the technical gift as their primary gift and another 8 percent listed it as their secondary gift.

DISCOVERING TECHNICAL GIFTS

Before considering what it looks like to share technical gifts in different areas of life and what it looks like to grow these gifts over time, first consider who in your life (including yourself!) may have technical gifts.

List people you know who may have technical gifts and what their specific gifting is (such as Tony—digitally mixing music).

Technical gifts *help you perform specific tasks that require a special and refined set of skills. Gifts include craftsmanship, profession-specific knowledge, and acquired skills.*

SHARING TECHNICAL GIFTS

While some technical gifts are developed and used in a professional setting (like the MIT scientist who listed "electronic and optical materials" on the survey), others are developed and used in nonwork settings (like Tony's digital music mixing). Technical gifts can be used to bless others and pursue the common good in many different areas of life.

To get a picture of what that could look like, let's consider the relevance of technical gifts to four different vocations in life. For each area we will also consider the case study of Terri. Terri is a car mechanic who has developed multiple technical gifts and uses them in a variety of places.

Family: The blessing of technical gifts within the household frequently goes overlooked. The variety of skills developed through specialized training or experience can not only improve the quality of life within a household but also help to reduce household expenses by providing services that would otherwise need to be paid for.

Terri has become the go-to mechanic for her large extended family, who all live in the same city. This isn't just a convenience for her family; in many cases, they wouldn't have the money to fix their cars or lawnmowers and would have to simply do without.

Church: The household of faith can benefit from the large variety of skills possessed by its members. Technical skills can benefit the members of the congregation and can also be used as key resources in a variety of outreach programs offered to the surrounding neighborhood and community.

When the pianist at Terri's church was taken out of commission for a few months because of a skiing accident, a call for pianists went out in the church bulletin. People were surprised when Terri (who it turns out has technical gifts in *music*, as well!) filled in wonderfully.

Work: Our occupational vocation is the most recognized context for the use of technical skills. The workplace is also the primary context where technical skills can be grown. As technical skills are developed for the workplace, new opportunities for personal advancement emerge along with more effective and efficient methods for achieving organizational vision and mission.

Terri's technical gifts with car repair are used daily in her work as an auto mechanic. Every day she works she is using the craftsmanship, profession-specific knowledge, and acquired skills that she has developed over time as she diagnoses what's wrong with the cars that are brought in and sets about fixing them.

Society: Our communities provide numerous opportunities to share our technical skills with our neighbors. When we share these abilities with others, we increase community cohesion and can directly affect neighborhood and community well-being. Using technical skills for service and mentorship in our communities creates a network of support and collaboration necessary for stability and growth.

Terri's neighbors have benefited in many ways because of her technical skills as a mechanic, helping them with their cars, lawnmowers, and more. And because Terri is willing to patiently explain what she is doing, she is informally helping others develop some of the acquired skills she has been honing her whole life.

Brainstorm ways to share technical gifts in each of these four areas. (Keep in mind the people you listed in the previous exercise.)

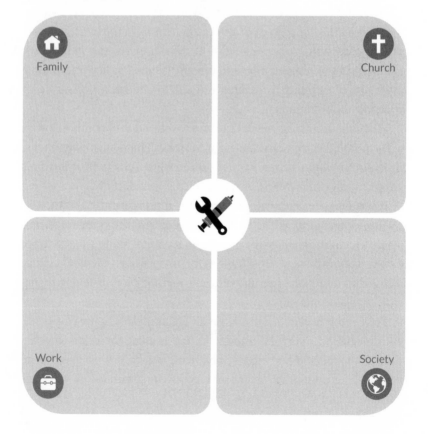

GROWING TECHNICAL GIFTS

An important part of stewarding the gifts that have been entrusted with us is investing time and energy in developing those gifts. Nationally, only 11 percent of those with technical gifts test as having achieved exemplary mastery of them, while 19 percent test as accomplished, and 70 percent are in the developing range.[2]

70%	19%	11%
DEVELOPING	ACCOMPLISHED	EXEMPLARY

For those who want to grow their technical gifts, there are three basic areas in which to pursue growth.

Craftsmanship involves demonstrating mastery-level skills in a particular craft. What does this look like in practice? Baz thoroughly enjoys creating pottery and ceramic home decor to sell through his small business. His craftmanship is apparent in the intricate details and simple aesthetic of the items he makes by hand.

Profession-specific knowledge involves possessing information and skills needed for a specific profession. An engineer by trade, Caris is talented in designing blueprints, deciding which materials to use for a project, and organizing the steps with which to complete a task. Caris's profession-specific knowledge allows her to manage a project well and achieve praiseworthy results.

Acquired skills involve developing new abilities through training or experience. What does that look like in practice? Isaac first expressed an interest in woodworking after years of watching his grandfather, a master carpenter, help neighbors and friends with home renovation projects. Now, after completing an apprenticeship, Isaac is ready to use his acquired skills professionally.

UNLEASHING TECHNICAL GIFTS

Our world needs everyone God has entrusted with technical gifts, like Tony, to use their gifts for the common good. The wide variety of technical gifts is a reminder of how important it is for all these gifts to be unleashed. Toward that end, remember to appreciate and celebrate technical gifts whenever you see them—whether in yourself or in others. This is one small way we can help unleash these important gifts.

Choose a specific person and vocation from the previous exercise and brainstorm ways the person could pursue growth in one or more of these three areas. (Remember to think about growth in knowledge, attitude, and skills.)

_____
has technical gifts.

Area to use their gift:
(circle one)

Family   Church

Work   Society

Brainstorm ways
to pursue growth:

Interpersonal Gifts

A soft answer turns away wrath, but a harsh word stirs up anger.

PROVERBS 15:1

People everywhere are the same; they are all people to be loved.
They are all hungry for love.

MOTHER TERESA, ALBANIAN-INDIAN NUN

Bobby, one of Don's high school friends, was something of a conundrum when Don first met him. A large Korean American teenager, he played lineman on the school's football team, yet he was one of the most kind, tender, personable people in the school.

When they first met, Don was a skinny, shy member of the school's speech team. He and Bobby couldn't have been more different. Yet because of Bobby's ability to befriend people and draw them out, the two quickly became friends. Bobby listened to, shared with, encouraged, and lifted up the people around him—not normal fare for a high school boy. Looking back, it is clear to Don that Bobby had been entrusted with tremendous interpersonal gifts.

These gifts (whether aptitudes, innate abilities, or acquired skills) manifest themselves differently in different people, of course. And while we all navigate relationships on a daily basis, there are some people, like Bobby, for whom these interpersonal gifts are a significant part of their lives.

Whether interpersonal gifts are your primary gift or not, it's important to recognize that *interpersonal gifts help you interact with, care for, and build relationships with others.* In our national survey, 10 percent of respondents listed interpersonal gifts as their primary gift, and another 10 percent listed them as their secondary gift.

DISCOVERING INTERPERSONAL GIFTS

Before considering what it looks like to share interpersonal gifts in different areas of life and what it looks like to *grow* these gifts over time, first consider who in your life (including yourself!) may have interpersonal gifts.

List people you know who may have interpersonal gifts.

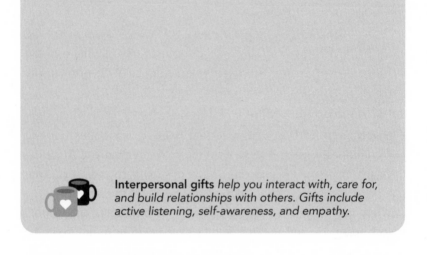

Interpersonal gifts *help you interact with, care for, and build relationships with others. Gifts include active listening, self-awareness, and empathy.*

SHARING INTERPERSONAL GIFTS

Relationships are an important part of almost every aspect of human life. (People are everywhere!) This means that interpersonal gifts are an invaluable asset in every area of life and can be shared fruitfully in many different ways.

Let's consider what it looks like to pursue the common good by sharing interpersonal gifts in four different contexts. For each area we will also consider the case study of Inez. Inez, a busy mother with four young children, actively uses her interpersonal gifts throughout the week.

Family: All households benefit from healthy relationships. The highly relational nature of the home is enhanced and deepened by its members' ability to share with and care for one another deeply. Working to grow and adapt interpersonal approaches within a household as it changes over time is key to keeping households safe, healthy, and happy.

Since Inez's mother was moved into a memory care facility, Inez has been visiting her regularly. Not only has Inez used her interpersonal gifts to love and care for her mother during these visits, but she has also been able to seed and nurture new relationships between her mother and a few of the other residents of the facility.

Church: The Christian church is all about relationships, beginning with members' relationship with God and expanding out through their congregation and community. The special interpersonal bond that Christians share as members of Jesus' one body is unique to all other human relationships. Striving to use interpersonal gifts within the diversity of the Christian church is not only import but is a hallmark of the Christian faith.

As a greeter in her home church, Inez greets members and guests alike, using her interpersonal gifts to make everyone feel welcomed, seen, and appreciated.

Work: Interpersonal skills help to bridge roles created by necessity in the workplace, which can sometimes feel artificial. These skills are important in overcoming the inevitable conflicts and divisions that occur as people work together under the pressure of their organization. Interpersonal skills deepen team relationships and help to provide the understanding and grace needed to achieve team goals.

At night when Inez's children are all in bed, she enjoys doing freelance graphic design jobs that engage her creative side and also help pay the bills. Inez's interpersonal gifts allow her to network fruitfully and produce a steady stream of new customers for her enjoyable side gig.

Society: Open and inclusive relationships within a community of diverse neighbors can only be achieved when interpersonal gifts are grown and shared. When the relational fabric of a community is strengthened by interpersonal gifts, the sense of belonging and the desire to participate among community members increases.

Anytime a new person or family moves into her neighborhood, Inez is quick to stop by with a plate of cookies to introduce herself, get to know her new neighbors, and help them meet others. In this way, Inez helps foster a sense of community in her neighborhood.

Brainstorm ways to share interpersonal gifts in each of these four areas. (Keep in mind the people you listed in the previous exercise.)

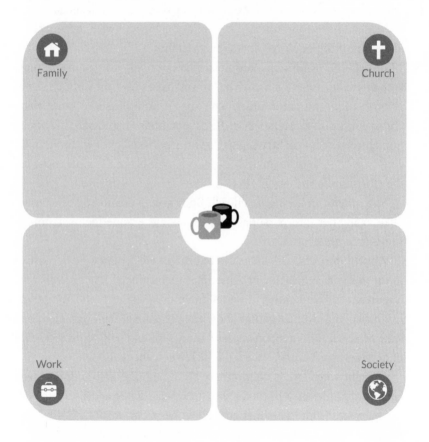

GROWING INTERPERSONAL GIFTS

Nationally, only 10 percent of those with interpersonal gifts test as having achieved exemplary mastery of them, while 18 percent test as accomplished, and 72 percent are in the developing range. For those who want to grow their interpersonal gifts, there are three basic areas in which to pursue growth.

72%
DEVELOPING

18%
ACCOMPLISHED

10%
EXEMPLARY

Active listening involves making a conscious effort to hear, reflect, and understand a message being communicated. What does this look like in practice? Arya is an amazing, heartfelt listener; her friends, family, and coworkers feel comfortable sharing all manner of stories with her. When someone needs to process something or share exciting news, Arya makes time to listen well, never judging, interjecting, changing the subject, or stealing the spotlight.

Self-awareness involves understanding one's own actions, thoughts, or emotions in relation to the environment and others. Whether working toward professional, academic, or personal goals, Malik's self-awareness allows him to accurately gauge where he currently stands in each realm and measure his capacity to grow. Understanding his emotions and limitations gives Malik confidence and energy to keep making positive changes in both himself and the world around him.

Empathy involves identifying with the feelings, thoughts, and experiences of another person. What does this look like in practice? Miriam is a school counselor whose empathy is used almost daily. An active and nonjudgmental listener, she is beloved by others and encourages those around her to practice empathy as well by listening, acknowledging, learning, and acting in the best interest of others.

UNLEASHING INTERPERSONAL GIFTS

Given how central relationships are to every aspect of human life, we all need to grow in our ability to relate with others. It is so vital, too, that everyone who has been entrusted with interpersonal gifts, like Don's friend Bobby, actively uses those gifts for the common good. Remember to appreciate and celebrate interpersonal gifts whenever you see them—whether in yourself or in others. This is one small way we can help unleash these important gifts.

Choose a specific person and vocation from the previous exercise and brainstorm ways the person could pursue growth in one or more of these three areas. (Remember to think about growth in knowledge, attitude, and skills.)

_____
has interpersonal gifts.

Area to use their gift:
(circle one)

Family   Church

Work   Society

Brainstorm ways
to pursue growth:

Entrepreneurial Gifts

*Behold, I am doing a new thing;
now it springs forth, do you not perceive it?*

ISAIAH 43:19

If opportunity doesn't knock, build a door.

MILTON BERLE, AMERICAN HUMORIST

Our friend Doug has been entrusted by God with considerable entrepreneurial gifts.

Don and Doug have worked together on a few different projects over the years, and Don noticed right away how many of their conversations began by Doug saying, "I had an idea . . ." or "What if we . . ." or "Would it be possible to . . . ." This is simply part of how Doug is made: he is always imagining new possibilities. And (just as important) he is quick to set tangible goals and design strategies to make those possibilities become a reality.

In fact, Doug's supervisor recently offered him the job (and title) of director of innovation. Doug wound up not taking that role, but the offer itself only affirms what we have seen firsthand: Doug can't help but imagine new opportunities and start figuring out how to pursue them. That's what entrepreneurial gifts are all about.

You don't have to work as a business entrepreneur for a living to have these gifts, of course. People in all sorts of occupations and life situations have entrepreneurial gifts (whether aptitudes, innate abilities, or acquired skills) and use them to benefit themselves and others. While these gifts come in a variety of expressions, they all have this in common: *entrepreneurial gifts help you identify new opportunities, set goals, and design strategies to achieve them.*

While many people have entrepreneurial gifts, there are some, like our friend Doug, for whom these gifts loom larger. In our national survey, 6 percent of respondents listed the entrepreneurial gift as their primary gift and another 6 percent listed it as their secondary gift.

DISCOVERING ENTREPRENEURIAL GIFTS

Our recent nationwide research revealed that not everyone is aware of the gifts entrusted to them. In addition, the research confirmed that people's awareness of their various gifts has a positive effect on their use of and development of those gifts.

So before considering what it looks like to share entrepreneurial gifts in different areas of life and what it looks like to grow these gifts over time, first consider who in your life (including yourself!) may have entrepreneurial gifts.

List people you know who may have entrepreneurial gifts.

Entrepreneurial gifts *help you identify new opportunities, set goals, and design strategies to achieve them. Gifts include analytical thinking, market research, marketing skills, problem-solving, and sales.*

SHARING ENTREPRENEURIAL GIFTS

While we may be most familiar with seeing entrepreneurial gifts expressed in the workforce (most obviously with business entrepreneurs), these God-given gifts can be used to bless others and pursue the common good in many different areas of life.

To get a picture of what that could look like, let's consider the relevance of entrepreneurial gifts to four different vocations in life. For each area we will also consider the case study of Eddie. Eddie is a fifteen-year-old who is already sharing his considerable entrepreneurial gifts in a variety of ways.

Family: Entrepreneurial gifts in the household can spawn a wide variety of opportunities for the advancement of the household. From the development of home-based businesses to the creation of a new approach to solving everyday household problems, entrepreneurial skills provide almost limitless possibilities.

Eddie's entire extended family gets together at a state park campground every summer for a week-long family reunion. When a steady rain threatened to spoil last year's reunion, Eddie concocted an entire Family Olympics on the spot, coming up with creative activities, teams, and even a memorable awards ceremony.

Church: Maintaining and growing a local congregation using entrepreneurial skills is important not only for the initial planting and launch of a congregation, but also for creatively achieving its mission in reaching out to those in the surrounding neighborhoods and communities. Professional and volunteer church leaders who possess these skills are a welcomed blessing to any congregation.

When Eddie was still a third grader, he noticed how many worship bulletins were being thrown away each Sunday. Eddie wrote up a detailed recycling proposal, and the leaders of the church took his proposal to heart. Now, less paper is going into landfills and other children are beginning to share their ideas with the church's leaders.

Work: Entrepreneurial gifts in the workplace are at the heart of new and creative business development and problem-solving. While these skills are normally seen as necessary to develop new endeavors, entrepreneurial eyes in existing organizations can help to see patterns, predict opportunities, and provide the vision and leadership needed to succeed in new ventures.

After a week at his new job at the local YMCA, Eddie was surprised by how many left-behind goggles, towels, and flip-flops had to be picked up and placed in the crowded and rarely checked lost and found box.

Eddie designed a new system in which lost items could be clipped to a very visible rope to be noticed and reunited with their owners.

Society: The vision and drive to innovate help move neighborhoods and communities forward by developing opportunities and initiatives that increase the common good. While ideas for improvement are helpful, entrepreneurial gifts help bring those ideas to life in a way that is both impactful and enduring.

A few years back, Eddie had the idea of holding an all-neighborhood garage sale—an event that has become an annual tradition for the neighborhood. Not only did he come up with the idea, but he had great insights as to how they could market the sale to bring in more traffic.

Brainstorm ways to share entrepreneurial gifts in each of these four areas. (Keep in mind the people you listed in the previous exercise.)

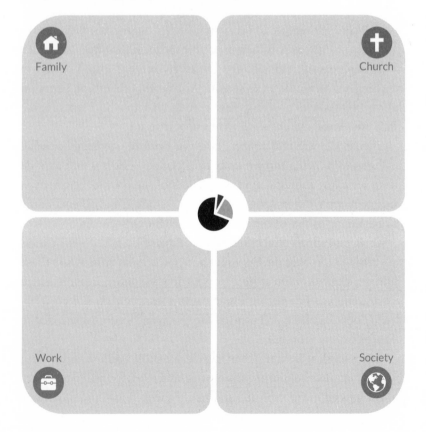

Family

Church

Work

Society

GROWING ENTREPRENEURIAL GIFTS

Nationally, only 14 percent of those with entrepreneurial gifts test as having achieved exemplary mastery of them, while 27 percent test as accomplished, and 59 percent are in the developing range.

59%	27%	14%
DEVELOPING	ACCOMPLISHED	EXEMPLARY

For those who want to grow their entrepreneurial gifts, there are five basic areas in which to pursue growth.

Analytical thinking involves breaking down complex information or data into basic parts or principles. What does this look like in practice? Lina is a front-end website developer who creates beautiful and efficient websites for her clients. When errors sometimes occur with programming or site layout, Lina uses analytical thinking to break the problem down step by step and chart a course of action to correct the issue.

Market research involves gathering and evaluating information about consumers' needs, preferences, and trends. A small-business owner in a bustling downtown area, Suci makes time to check in with her customer base regularly. She also keeps up with the latest trends in women's wear. Suci's tactical use of market research allows her to keep her current patrons satisfied while adding new visitors to her boutique's loyal customer base.

Marketing skills involve strategically promoting a product, service, or idea to a target audience. What does this look like in practice? Rai is a marketing manager at a small, international publishing company. Daily, whether or not he is on the job, Rai exercises his tactical and planning skills to come up with the best processes for getting his company's books into the hands of their intended audience. Rai is skilled at positioning products to succeed.

Problem-solving involves investigating a problem to determine its source and an effective solution. As a manager at a tech company, Sharon is constantly problem-solving alongside her teammates as they tweak code and redesign facets of digital products. Sharon is energized by these daily tasks; in her opinion, there is no greater feeling than pushing through a problem to the discovery of a solution.

Sales involves utilizing product knowledge to meet customers' needs through providing products and services. Isla works at a wholesale boat shop that stocks everything from new propellers to used drain plugs. As a sales representative, Isla works with customers to determine their needs or wants before informing them of items that she believes will best meet their needs.

UNLEASHING ENTREPRENEURIAL GIFTS

Our world needs everyone God has entrusted with entrepreneurial gifts, like our friend Doug, to use their gifts for the common good. Without these important gifts, our organizations and lives and society will surely stagnate over time. So remember to appreciate and celebrate entrepreneurial gifts whenever you see them—whether in yourself or in others. This is one small way we can help unleash these important gifts.

Choose a specific person and vocation from the previous exercise and brainstorm ways the person could pursue growth in one or more of these five areas. (Remember to think about growth in knowledge, attitude, and skills.)

_____
has entrepreneurial gifts.

Area to use their gift:
(circle one)

🏠 ✝
Family Church

💼 🌍
Work Society

Brainstorm ways to pursue growth:

Management Gifts

*Now Solomon purposed to build a temple for the name
of the Lord, and a royal palace for himself. And Solomon
assigned 70,000 men to bear burdens and 80,000 to
quarry in the hill country, and 3,600 to oversee them.*

2 CHRONICLES 2:1-2

*Of all the things I've done, the most vital is coordinating the talents
of those who work for us and pointing them toward a certain goal.*

WALT DISNEY, AMERICAN ENTERTAINER

As former pastors, the two of us have been a part of many Vacation Bible Schools (VBS) over the years. We love these much-anticipated summer events and what they do for those in the church and in the surrounding community.

And while the theme of VBS changes every year, one thing never changes: the need to manage a high number of volunteers and tasks. The building and grounds need to be prepared; teachers and station leaders need to be trained and mobilized; parent release statements and health information paperwork need to be organized, collected, and filed.

From song leaders to snack preparers to photo takers to Band-Aid dispensers . . . it takes lots of tasks and people to pull off a successful VBS. This is where management gifts come in. Whether you are managing a business, department, team, or VBS, *management gifts help you manage both tasks and people.*

While we all have to manage tasks and people from time to time, there are some people who have special aptitudes, innate abilities, or acquired skills that help them manage in especially fruitful ways. In a national survey, 6 percent of respondents listed the management gift as their primary gift, and another 7 percent listed it as their secondary gift.

DISCOVERING MANAGEMENT GIFTS

Before considering what it looks like to share management gifts in different areas of life and what it looks like to grow these gifts over time, first consider who in your life (including yourself!) may have management gifts.

List people you know who may have management gifts.

Management gifts *help you manage both tasks and people. Gifts include decision-making, project planning, task delegation, and communication.*

SHARING MANAGEMENT GIFTS

Because manager is an actual role that many people hold in the business world, it can be tempting to associate management gifts with the workplace alone. The reality is that management gifts are crucial in many areas of life.

Let's consider the relevance of management gifts in four areas. For each area we will also consider the case study of Melinda. Melinda is an empty nester, a grandmother who has served in a long career as a chef. Though most people notice Melinda's technical and artistic gifts as a chef, she also has considerable management gifts that she shares in a variety of ways.

Family: Managing a household is in many ways the basis for all management in society. While the necessity and complexity of management gifts are frequently underappreciated, they are at the heart of every home. The management of time, money, resources, and people fill calendars and checkbooks. Although sometimes underemphasized, the art of managing a home and its economics remains important.

Melinda's extended family has always gravitated to her home for their holiday family gatherings. Coordinating the schedules, potluck offerings, chores, and fun activities might stress someone else out, but Melinda's way with project planning, task delegation, and communication have always made for stress-free family gatherings.

Church: Managing both the ministry and the business aspects of a congregation can be a daunting task involving a variety of management gifts. Without proper management of both areas, neither will be stable or successful. Because many professional church leaders are more trained in ministry skills than management skills, successful ministry may require members with management gifts to share those gifts within the church.

Every year Melinda's church runs a month-long stewardship campaign. Since Melinda joined the stewardship committee, all the fairly complex tasks involved (clarifying vision, creating print pieces, collecting and recording pledges) have been managed more efficiently, and the annual campaign has been more effective.

Work: Management gifts in the workplace are at the heart of organizational health and stability. While the outward-facing aspects of an organization's mission frequently get the attention and praise, management gifts ensure that an organization has a strong and solid foundation to support the development and delivery of products and services. Equity, accountability, and efficiency all increase when these gifts are shared.

If you've ever spent time in a busy commercial kitchen, you know that decision-making, task delegation, and communication are crucial to a well-run kitchen. Melinda has strengths in all three of these skills, allowing her kitchen to thrive over the years.

Society: The importance of managing neighborhood and community resources is a growing area of study in community development. Increasing a community's well-being involves more than the creation of new projects or possibilities. Skillful management helps connect community resources to those who need them most.

Many people love attending a block party in their neighborhood, but not everyone is thrilled to help plan and pull off such a large event. Melinda, however, has loved volunteering on the planning committee as she shares her management gifts (along with her deviled eggs!) with her neighborhood.

Brainstorm ways to share management gifts in each of these four areas. (Keep in mind the people you listed in the previous exercise.)

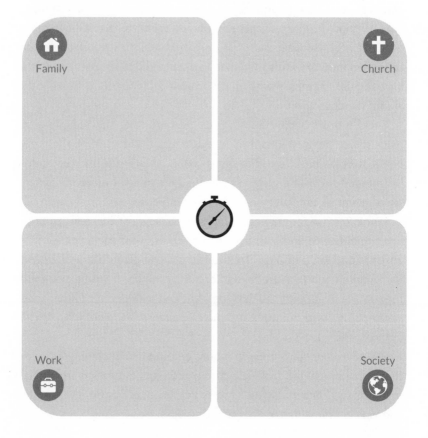

Family

Church

Work

Society

GROWING MANAGEMENT GIFTS

Nationally, only 17 percent of those with management gifts test as having achieved exemplary mastery of them, while 25 percent test as accomplished, and 58 percent are in the developing range.

58%	25%	17%
DEVELOPING	ACCOMPLISHED	EXEMPLARY

For those who want to grow their management gifts, there are four basic areas in which to pursue growth.

Decision-making involves determining a course of action from several possibilities by weighing options and outcomes. What does this look like in practice? Paz directs a daycare, and with so many workers and children to oversee, she has become quite good at exercising her decision-making skills. Whether it's thinking through a new craft for the toddlers or figuring out how to keep everything running smoothly when short-staffed, Paz weighs all the options and outcomes before making an informed choice and confidently leading her team forward.

Project planning involves describing the cost, scope, and schedule of a project to effectively meet project goals. Every spring and fall, Melanie puts her project planning skills to use as she organizes a fundraiser for the nonprofit where she volunteers. This requires attention to detail, flexibility, time management, and organization. Melanie dedicates months to planning these events each year, ensuring that the fundraisers will go off without a hitch.

Task delegation involves assigning authority and responsibility for particular functions, tasks, or decisions to another person. The head of a construction team that spends most of its time repairing highways, Liam spends many hours problem-solving and delegating tasks to the group he oversees. With his knowledge of the workers and skill sets on his team, Liam knows to whom he should delegate each task in order to quickly, safely, and efficiently finish the job.

Communication involves sending and receiving messages through verbal and nonverbal means in order to convey a clear meaning. Akeno is talented at explaining things to others in a clear and thoughtful way. He often relies on body language to emphasize the message he's trying to get across. Akeno is a good communicator who effortlessly gets everyone on the same page.

UNLEASHING MANAGEMENT GIFTS

Our world needs everyone God has entrusted with management gifts to use their gifts for the common good. Little in life would continue to get done were it not for these important but often behind-the-scenes gifts. So remember to appreciate and celebrate management gifts whenever you see them—whether in yourself or in others. This is one small way we can help unleash these important gifts.

Choose a specific person and vocation from the previous exercise and brainstorm ways the person could pursue growth in one or more of these four areas. (Remember to think about growth in knowledge, attitude, and skills.)

_____
has management gifts.

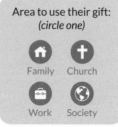

Area to use their gift:
(circle one)

Family   Church

Work   Society

Brainstorm ways
to pursue growth:

Financial Gifts

> *Which of you, desiring to build a tower,*
> *does not first sit down and count the cost,*
> *whether he has enough to complete it?*
>
> **LUKE 14:28**

> *Money is a terrible master but an excellent servant.*
>
> **P. T. BARNUM, AMERICAN ENTERTAINER**

In a world with calculators and spreadsheets and banking apps and electronic tax-filing, is there really any need for financial gifts? The short answer is—absolutely!

It doesn't matter how much great and helpful technology we bring to bear on our individual or corporate handling of finances, there will always be a need for people who have the accounting skills, planning instincts, and attention to detail it takes to handle finances well.

Every area of life involves finances in one way or another: our households, churches, and workplaces—even most of our teams, clubs, schools, and associations—have some sort of budget or finances that need to be handled well. This means all of us need to develop some measure of facility with handling money, whether we have gifts for it or not.

But some people have been entrusted with special aptitudes, innate abilities, and acquired skills in the area of finances. *Financial gifts help you plan, organize, direct, and control financial activities.* While everyone has to deal with finances, 7 percent of respondents in a nationwide survey listed the financial gift as their primary gift. Another 9 percent listed it as their secondary gift.

DISCOVERING FINANCIAL GIFTS

Before considering what it looks like for those with financial gifts to share those gifts in different areas of life and grow those gifts over time, we invite you to consider who in your life (including yourself!) may have financial gifts.

List people you know who may have financial gifts.

Financial gifts *help you plan, organize, direct, and control financial activities. Gifts include accounting, planning, and attention to detail.*

SHARING FINANCIAL GIFTS

Although financial gifts may seem very specific and narrow in scope, the reality is aptitudes, innate abilities, and acquired skills in the area of finances can be used for the common good in all areas of life.

To get a picture of what that could look like, let's consider the relevance of financial gifts to four different callings in life. For each area we will also consider the case study of Frances. Frances is a retired tax accountant whose financial gifts have impacted and blessed many people in her life.

Family: The need for financial gifts within the household is obvious, as money is one of the biggest stressors in home life. But the complexities of finances in an ever-changing economic environment can't be overstated. The presence of financial gifts can make a huge difference in household planning, education, and retirement.

Although Frances's sister, Lydia, made fun of her for studying "boring" accounting in college, when Lydia's start-up business failed, she had to confess to Frances that she had run up a huge debt and was contemplating bankruptcy. Frances's ability to plan, organize, and control financial activities wound up saving the day for Lydia.

Church: Fundraising, stewardship, and the accounting of ministry funds are all aspects of ministry that can benefit from financial gifts. While the relationship between money and ministry is sometimes seen as a taboo topic, successful ministries acknowledge that the two go hand in hand. In many ways, finances are not separate from ministry but are a ministry in and of themselves.

Frances's church is required by its bylaws to get someone outside the accounting staff to do an audit of their books each year. Instead of having the church pay an outside firm to perform the audit, Frances offered to do the work herself—an act of stewardship that has enriched Frances's sense of involvement with her church.

Work: Almost every aspect of our occupational lives is impacted by finances. Salaries, budgets, endowments, and investments are but a few areas where financial gifts can be helpful in the workplace. While not all organizations are focused on making profits, all organizations need the appropriate financial gifts necessary to keep an organization healthy and accountable.

In her work as a tax accountant, Frances was able to use her considerable abilities in accounting, planning, and attention to detail on a daily basis for decades. As tax laws changed over time, Frances invested in keeping her accounting skills sharp and up to date.

Society: Financial gifts shared and developed within a community can help a community and its members flourish and grow. Our local communities represent economic microcosms. Many of the same gifts needed in the economy as a whole are also needed in the local economy. Helping individual communities achieve financial health results in a cumulative impact that affects the surrounding region and even the nation.

When Frances found out that the leader of her neighborhood association, Sam, was stressed by having to keep track of all of the finances of the association, the newly retired Frances was more than happy to use her gifts to take that task off Sam's hands, freeing him up to use his leadership gifts more.

Brainstorm ways to share financial gifts in each of these four areas. (Keep in mind the people you listed in the previous exercise.)

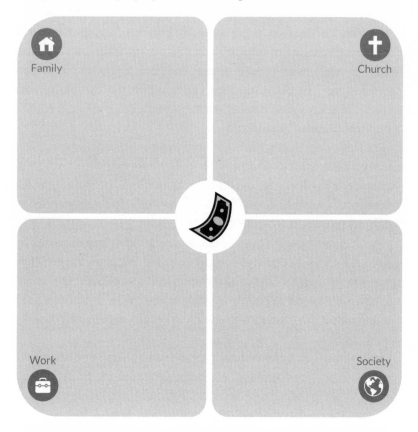

GROWING FINANCIAL GIFTS

An important part of stewarding the gifts that have been entrusted to us is investing time and energy in developing those gifts. Nationally only 17 percent of those with financial gifts test as having achieved exemplary mastery of them, while 24 percent test as accomplished, and 59 percent are in the developing range.

59%	24%	17%
DEVELOPING	ACCOMPLISHED	EXEMPLARY

For those who want to grow their financial gifts, there are three basic areas in which to pursue growth.

Accounting involves recording, analyzing, and reporting financial transactions. What does this look like in practice? Tyler's strength has always been in mathematics and finance. After graduating from college, he found a job at an accounting firm. Tyler uses his strength to manage the financial records of companies. He spends his working hours ensuring that his clients' finances are allotted and spent in a way that will strengthen their business.

Planning involves preparing short- and long-term plans to accomplish specific financial goals. Mei loves to plan ahead, especially when it comes to finances. At the end of every week, Mei looks over her monthly budget to ensure she's on track, making adjustments when needed. Mei's financial foresight has also led her to write a five- and ten-year plan as well as invest in both mutual funds and the stock market.

Attention to detail involves focusing on specific details to achieve thoroughness and accuracy. Sarah uses an app on her phone to track every dollar she spends. She finds great peace and comfort in knowing exactly how she is stewarding her finances. She uses this gifting to serve her church by being the trustworthy volunteer who counts the offering money each week.

UNLEASHING FINANCIAL GIFTS

When our money gets out of control or mismanaged, stressors multiply. This is why we need everyone God has entrusted with financial gifts to use their gifts for the common good. Toward that end, make a point to appreciate and celebrate financial gifts whenever you see them—whether in yourself or in others. This is one small way we can help unleash these important gifts.

Choose a specific person and vocation from the previous exercise, and brainstorm ways the person could pursue growth in one or more of these three areas. (Remember to think about growth in knowledge, attitude, and skills.)

_____
has financial gifts.

Area to use their gift:
(circle one)

Family   Church

Work   Society

Brainstorm ways
to pursue growth:

Critical Thinking Gifts

> *The simple believes everything,*
> *but the prudent gives thought to his steps.*
> **PROVERBS 14:15**

> *It's not that I'm so smart, it's just that*
> *I stay with problems longer.*
> **ALBERT EINSTEIN, GERMAN PHYSICIST**

At **Lutheran Hour Ministries** we use research to inform our ministries, strategies, and resources. We work with the Barna Group to perform fairly involved nationwide research each year, which means we wind up with a considerable amount of data to process.

It's not enough, we've found, to get data. You then have to process that data using critical thinking, creativity, data analytics, and decision-making. Our team has been known to spend hours a day for weeks at a time in a room with four dry-erase walls trying to make sense of the research findings. During those think-tank times, critical thinking gifts especially come in handy.

You don't have to be doing nationwide research to use critical thinking gifts, of course. Life is filled with opportunities to use these gifts. *Critical thinking gifts help you process data to problem-solve or make informed decisions.* From tasks as small as making a household decision (what car to buy, which job to apply for, where to invest your savings) to tasks as big as setting an organization's vision and strategies, critical thinking gifts are a huge blessing.

While many people have critical thinking gifts, there are some people, like some of our friends at Lutheran Hour Ministries and the Barna Group, for whom these gifts are a bigger part of their lives. In a national survey, more people chose critical thinking gifts as their primary gifts than any other gift type—12 percent of respondents listing the critical thinking gift as their primary gift and another 11 percent listed it as their secondary gift.

DISCOVERING CRITICAL THINKING GIFTS

It's important to consider what it looks like to share critical thinking gifts in different areas of life and what it looks like to grow these gifts over time. But first consider who in your life (including yourself!) may have critical thinking gifts.

List people you know who may have critical thinking gifts.

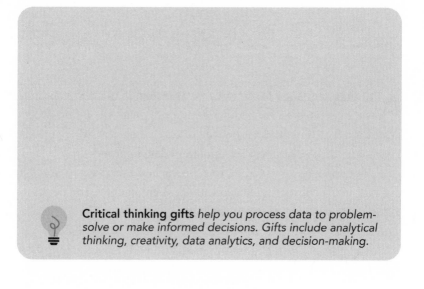

Critical thinking gifts *help you process data to problem-solve or make informed decisions. Gifts include analytical thinking, creativity, data analytics, and decision-making.*

SHARING CRITICAL THINKING GIFTS

Critical thinking is something we do almost every day of our lives—or at least it is something we should do! The ability to process data to problem-solve or make informed decisions comes in handy in many different contexts, so it is a huge blessing when those with critical thinking gifts generously share those gifts.

Let's consider the relevance of critical thinking gifts to four different vocations in life. For each area we will also consider the case study of Christopher. Christopher is a middle school teacher, husband, and father of two teenagers, and his critical thinking gifts have affected and blessed many people in his life.

Family: In an environment in which the heart leads, critical thinking brings clarity of thought and the ability to solve problems in a reasoned way. Each household is faced with numerous dilemmas and decisions that can be aided by a critical and reasoned approach to the facts and context. These gifts brings the blessing of the ability to take a step back and see the big picture and its moving parts in order to discover a way forward.

Christopher's critical thinking gifts have been essential in helping his family navigate the quickly changing landscape of technology, social media, and cultural norms. He helps the family process an influx of information about emerging technologies and make some informed, wise decisions about how they will handle screens as a family.

Church: Since a congregation is comprised of many people, there are many opinions and perspectives to consider. Without the gift of critical thinking, congregational decisions and actions can be unduly influenced by personality, status, or personal perspective. Critical thinking provides for a thorough analysis of the issue at hand in order to find solutions that are faithful and benefit the ministry as a whole.

Christopher has served two years of a three-year term on his church's elder board. Not only does he enjoy the monthly meetings, but he loves reading and digesting the reports all elders are supposed to read prior to the meetings. Christopher's grasp of the details of the reports often helps the group come to a consensus on an issue.

Work: In the work environment it is easy to perform our daily tasks without fully understanding why we perform them or how they fit into the organization's strategic priorities. Critical thinking can help to analyze processes, plans, policies, and procedures to make sure that the individual efforts of team members work together and that organizational goals are achieved.

One important aspect of Christopher's job as a middle school teacher is adapting his curriculum to students who have individualized education plans (IEPs). Christopher's critical thinking skills have made him a go-to consultant with fellow teachers on how to process these sometimes long and complex IEPs.

Society: The ability to carefully think through complex community issues by considering available data within a local context is one of the many benefits that critical thinking brings to a neighborhood. Critical thinking helps to elevate issues and conversations to a level that allows the pursuit of the common good instead of the benefit of select community members.

During Christopher's two weeks on jury duty, he provided helpful questions, thoughts, and insights during group deliberation. Though he was not the leader of the jury, Christopher's ability to process data, help make decisions, and solve problems was a huge asset to the whole jury.

Brainstorm ways to share critical thinking gifts in each of these four areas. (Keep in mind the people you listed in the previous exercise.)

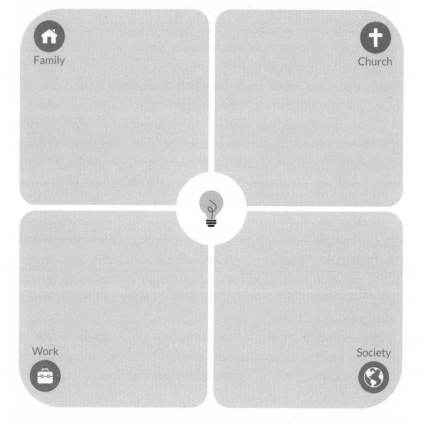

Family

Church

Work

Society

GROWING CRITICAL THINKING GIFTS

Nationally, only 17 percent of those with critical thinking gifts test as having achieved exemplary mastery of them, while 25 percent test as accomplished, and 58 percent are in the developing range.

58%	25%	17%
DEVELOPING	ACCOMPLISHED	EXEMPLARY

For those who want to grow their critical thinking gifts, there are four basic areas in which to pursue growth.

Analytical thinking involves breaking down complex information or data into basic parts or principles. What does this look like in practice? Lina is a front-end website developer who creates beautiful and efficient websites for her clients. When errors sometimes occur with programming or site layout, Lina uses analytical thinking to break the problem down step by step and chart a course of action to correct the issue for clients and their customers.

Creativity involves generating or connecting ideas in new and imaginative ways. Rico likes to think outside the box, especially when it comes to teaching science to his fourth-grade students. To enhance the prebuilt curriculum his school uses, Rico plans ahead to discover new and creative ways for the students to engage in hands-on learning.

Data analytics involve analyzing raw data to look for insights or trends. Diamond takes pride in being data-informed as she creates a vivid social media presence for all her clients. Using a variety of data-collecting apps, Diamond keeps a close eye on digital engagement rates for all accounts she monitors, allowing the findings to inform future posts and campaigns.

Decision-making involves determining a course of action from several possibilities by weighing options and outcomes. What does this look like in practice? Paz directs a daycare, and with so many workers and children to oversee, she has become quite good at exercising her decision-making skills. Whether it's thinking through a new craft for the toddlers or figuring out how to keep everything running smoothly when short-staffed, Paz weighs all the options and outcomes before making an informed choice and confidently leading her team forward.

UNLEASHING CRITICAL THINKING GIFTS

Given how complex our world is becoming and how quickly changes are blossoming all around us, it is paramount that everyone who has been entrusted with critical thinking gifts use their gifts for the good of as many people around them as possible. So be sure to appreciate and celebrate critical thinking gifts whenever you see them—whether in yourself or in others. This is one small way we can help unleash these important gifts.

Choose a specific person and vocation from the previous exercise and brainstorm ways the person could pursue growth in one or more of these four areas. (Remember to think about growth in knowledge, attitude, and skills.)

Artistic Gifts

> All the craftsmen among the workmen made the tabernacle with
> ten curtains. They were made of fine twined linen and blue and
> purple and scarlet yarns, with cherubim skillfully worked.
>
> **EXODUS 36:8**

> I found I could say things with color and shapes that
> I couldn't say any other way—things I had no words for.
>
> **GEORGIA O'KEEFFE, AMERICAN ARTIST**

Don's daughter, Teya, was still in diapers when he and his wife, Wendy, started to wonder whether perhaps God had given her some artistic gifts. They were on a summer road trip in a car without air conditioning, so Teya was in her car seat with only her diaper on. Don and Wendy were enjoying a long, uninterrupted conversation in the front seats (each grateful for how quiet the kids were being in the back) only to discover when they stopped for gas why Teya, at least, was being so quiet.

It turns out Teya had found a ballpoint pen and had decorated every square inch of her skin (except her left arm which held the pen) with intricate, evenly spaced, vine-like designs. Don and Wendy were upset that they had left a pen within her reach but were pretty enthralled by what she had created! These designs weren't the normal scribbles you'd expect from a toddler. And they were just the beginning—Teya went on to paint, draw, sculpt, and design her way all the way to art school.

While Teya's artistic gifts are manifested in the literal creation of art, many others express their artistic gifts in music, writing, and dance. Even disciplines like engineering, architecture, and gardening employ artistic gifts: *artistic gifts help you express yourself in creative and artistic ways.*

While many people have artistic gifts, there are some people, like Teya, for whom these gifts are a bigger part of their lives. In a national survey, 11 percent of respondents listed the artistic gift as their primary gift and another 7 percent listed it as their secondary gift.

DISCOVERING ARTISTIC GIFTS

We are going to examine what it looks like to share artistic gifts in different areas of life and what it looks like to grow these gifts over time, but first consider who in your life (including yourself!) may have artistic gifts.

List people you know who may have artistic gifts.

Artistic gifts *help you express yourself in creative and artistic ways. Gifts include all forms of artistic expression, media use, design, composition, and performance.*

SHARING ARTISTIC GIFTS

Artistic gifts may not always seem commercially fruitful ("starving artist" is a cliché for a reason!), but they are unquestionably spiritually and emotionally and mentally fruitful. As Spanish artist Pablo Picasso put it, "The purpose of art is washing the dust of daily life off our souls." This is why we need those with artistic gifts to share those gifts in every area of life.

To get a picture of what that could look like, let's consider the relevance of artistic gifts in four distinct areas of life. For each area we will also consider the case study of Auntie Annette. Annette isn't an actual aunt (she was an only child), but everyone who gets to know Annette winds up calling her "auntie" and being blessed by her considerable artistic gifts—no matter where they run into her.

Family: Artistic gifts within the household come in a variety of forms. Creating an aesthetically pleasing environment through art, crafts, decorating, gardening, music, and puppet shows in the backyard all find their source in artistic gifts. Creating a household environment that artistically stimulates the senses brings wonder, joy, and creativity.

Annette's parents arrived in the United States as refugees, and the emotional wounds of the civil war they lived through never completely went away. What a joyful and healing blessing, then, when their daughter, Annette, began decorating their house at an early age with brightly colored pictures, paintings, and sculptures.

Church: Artistic gifts are a wonderful tool to aid in the proclamation of the gospel narrative. Congregations have historically been a center for gospel-based artistic expression in stained glass, woodcuts, paintings, music, dance, theater, poetry, illustration, and more. For every artistic expression, there is an opportunity to use it to tell the story of Jesus and give glory to God.

The children's ministry team at her church just loves Auntie Annette. Every summer she helps design and create the unique staging and themed decorations for Vacation Bible School.

Work: Every organization represents its mission and message through art. Videos, graphic design, logos, jingles, and even interior design are utilized in the workplace. Depending on one's artistic gift, there is most likely an opportunity to make use of that gift at work, either formally as part of one's role or informally to assist in decorating and beautifying the workplace.

Auntie Annette has waited tables at Central Café for over thirty years. When she first started there she began folding napkins in creative ways; soon return customers were disappointed if they didn't get one of her napkins. Over time, Annette was also asked to create seasonal window art and write the specials on the large chalkboard—giving Central Café a unique vibe that keeps customers coming back.

Society: Murals, statues, concerts, architecture, art shows, and community art projects all benefit from artistic gifts. Art within neighborhoods and communities can be used to remember, inspire, and bring a sense of community identity and joy. Art within communities can be found in local galleries as well as adorning the sides of buildings, expressing deep community emotion and meaning.

Everyone who lives on Auntie Annette's block loves how she expresses herself creatively with handmade lawn ornaments, fascinating sculptures, and ever-changing window art to fit the season. Auntie's house brightens everyone's mood when they walk or drive by, and neighborhood children love to make crafts on her porch.

Brainstorm ways to share artistic gifts in each of these four areas. (Keep in mind the people you listed in the previous exercise.)

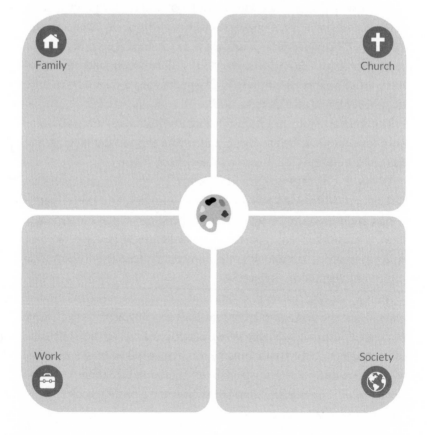

Family

Church

Work

Society

GROWING ARTISTIC GIFTS

Nationally, only 18 percent of those with artistic gifts test as having achieved exemplary mastery of them, while 26 percent test as accomplished, and 56 percent are in the developing range.

56%	26%	18%
DEVELOPING	ACCOMPLISHED	EXEMPLARY

For those who want to grow their artistic gifts, there are five basic areas in which to pursue growth.

Artistic expression involves reflecting one's thoughts, feelings, and experiences by representing internal visions in external forms. What does this look like in practice? Tevin's favorite place to be is behind a camera lens. Seeing the world through the viewfinder of his camera helps him focus on specific places, people, and actions that inspire his creativity. Tevin loves to use his gifting to tell stories visually.

Media use involves utilizing materials and tools in an artistic way. As an up-and-coming film student, Elin spends a lot of her time studying the different ways she can use media to tell stories or share a message. When thinking through a story line, Elin thinks about the kind of medium and narrative she wants to use, always keeping her audience in mind, before setting out to film.

Design involves constructing a plan prior to creating something. From InDesign to Photoshop, Lexi's knowledge of design platforms and techniques allow her to create vivid, stunning, and effective content for her client. She can create printable flyers, website pages, and everything in between. Designing strong, beautiful content in fresh ways is Lexi's passion.

Composition involves arranging various components in an aesthetically pleasing way. Urri is a beatmaker who uses various samples and software to create tracks that vocalists and other recording artists can use in their projects. Urri's knowledge of music theory and audio engineering as well as his innate sense of rhythm empower him to compose dynamic and emotive pieces of music that make people come alive.

Performance involves embodying a presentation of art or skill for an audience. Cara has always loved singing and has a beautiful voice, which led her to attend a liberal arts college for vocal performance. During college and even after graduating, Cara learned that a good performance is not based solely on one's talent but also on how one connects with the audience. Learning this enabled Cara to excel in her skill and build a career for herself as a vocal artist.

UNLEASHING ARTISTIC GIFTS

We all need to "wash the dust of daily life off our souls" from time to time, and that's why we need everyone God has entrusted with artistic gifts, like Teya, to use their gifts for the common good. Artistic gifts aren't always commercially rewarded, so let's do what we can to appreciate and celebrate artistic gifts whenever we see them—whether in ourselves or in others. This is one small way we can help unleash these important gifts.

Choose a specific person and vocation from the previous exercise and brainstorm ways the person could pursue growth in one or more of these five areas. (Remember to think about growth in knowledge, attitude, and skills.)

_____
has artistic gifts.

Area to use their gift:
(circle one)

🏠 ✝
Family   Church

💼 🌍
Work   Society

Brainstorm ways
to pursue growth:

Civic Gifts

*Seek the welfare of the city
where I have sent you.*
JEREMIAH 29:7

*Every so often, in the midst of chaos,
you come across an amazing, inexplicable
instance of civic responsibility.*
KURT VONNEGUT, AMERICAN WRITER

We are part of a new collaborative network committed to improving neighborhood well-being called The Hopeful Neighborhood Project. The resources and online network equip and encourage neighbors to work together, using their gifts and the gifts of their community to pursue the good of the neighborhood.

Being a part of this network has caused us both to have an increased appreciation for civic gifts. *Civic gifts help you make an impact by participating as a citizen within an organized community.*

The Hopeful Neighborhood Project has a neighborhood coach, Sara, who epitomizes these important civic gifts. Sara has a mix of aptitudes, innate abilities, and acquired skills that help her winsomely and fruitfully make a difference in her neighborhood and surrounding community. Sara's civic gifts help her coach others who want to do the same. Of the twelve gift areas we are exploring, civic gifts are perhaps the least noticed. Only 4 percent of Americans list this as their primary gift and 5 percent as their secondary gift—a much smaller number than shown in the other twelve gift areas.

DISCOVERING CIVIC GIFTS

While some families and communities talk about civic engagement a lot, other families and communities rarely do at all. To learn more about these gifts we are going to consider what it looks like to share civic gifts in different areas of life and what it looks like to grow these gifts over time. But first, consider who in your life (including yourself!) may have civic gifts.

List people you know who may have civic gifts.

Civic gifts *help you make an impact by participating as a citizen within an organized community. Gifts include advocacy, knowledge of political systems, and the ability to critically think about civic and political life.*

SHARING CIVIC GIFTS

Civic gifts may be the least recognized in our study, but they are by no means the least important. We all live within organized communities. Even those living in remote rural areas are a part of a county and a state and a country. Because we all live in organized communities, we need those with civic gifts to share those gifts in every area of their lives.

Let's consider the specific relevance of civic gifts in four areas of life. For each area we will also consider the case study of Charlie. Only nineteen years old, Charlie has already developed a reputation for being well versed in civic matters, and his political instincts have blessed a variety of people in his life.

Family: Civic gifts can help members of a household understand their civic responsibilities and the impact that civic affairs can have on the household. Voting, zoning, taxes, community leadership, and equitable representation are key areas in which civic gifts can be shared and developed.

Charlie's extended family has always been vocal about politics—sometimes in really heated ways. Charlie's knowledge of political systems has been a blessing to all in his family as he has begun to insert calm facts and data into their conversations, helping them become less rhetorical and more factual and respectful.

Church: Most congregations function under a specific organizational or denominational form that informs how they are led and governed. Congregations also provide a number of opportunities to partner with civil authorities to address local and community issues. In many places, churches and their leadership not only have the opportunity but the expectation that they will partner and participate in civil affairs.

When Charlie's new pastor introduced Robert's Rules of Order as a new way to conduct church meetings, members grew frustrated. Charlie helped people understand how the rules were designed to create healthy checks and balances, calming everyone and averting a potential crisis in the life of the new pastor.

Work: All businesses work within community, state, and federal policies and regulations. Knowing how to adhere to and advocate for civic policies and procedures that adequately represent the community is a part of the responsibility community organizations and businesses share. Businesses and organizations can play a powerful role in gaining a hearing for perspectives that an individual alone might struggle to accomplish.

In his work at Dell's Pizza Parlor, Charlie has done more than deliver pizzas. He has also helped the owners expand their business by building an outside patio area. When his employer ran into red tape with the local government, Charlie researched the relevant zoning laws and helped figure out the way forward.

Society: Local civic leadership and organization impacts almost every aspect of community life. Participating in civic responsibilities and opportunities strengthens the community. Civic gifts can be used to help a local community embrace its larger civic roles and responsibilities in relation to the larger state and federal contexts to ensure they are represented and receive the resources they need.

Charlie's family may live in one of the older neighborhoods in town, but they have the nicest, newest sidewalks. During a ninth-grade unit on civic responsibility, instead of writing a final paper, Charlie used his growing civic gifts to raise the awareness, political will, and supplemental funds it took to replace the aging sidewalks.

Brainstorm ways to share civic gifts in each of these four areas. (Keep in mind the people you listed in the previous exercise.)

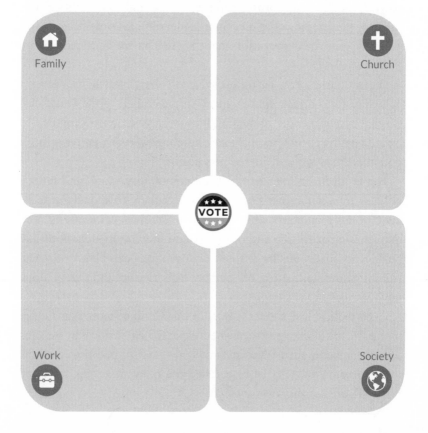

GROWING CIVIC GIFTS

Nationally, only 18 percent of those with civic gifts test as having achieved exemplary mastery of them, while 28 percent test as accomplished, and 54 percent are in the developing range.

54%	28%	18%
DEVELOPING	ACCOMPLISHED	EXEMPLARY

For those who want to grow their civic gifts, there are three basic areas in which to pursue growth.

Advocacy involves speaking on behalf of a person, group, cause, or policy in the public realm. What does this look like in practice? Aisha has a heart for advocacy; she longs to amplify the voices of others or speak up for those who have no voice. Throughout the year, she rallies her friends and other members of the community to speak out against injustices or inequities in the community.

Knowledge of political systems involves possessing an understanding of how local, state, and federal institutions and processes affect the individual and their neighborhood. Having spent years as a campaign manager for a local politician, Ken now spends his retirement years visiting high schools and colleges to speak to young people about the importance of voting. Ken built his career on his knowledge of political systems, which now allows him to inform others about how they can play a part in shaping the nation and history.

The ability to think critically about civic and political life involves processing civic information in order to make decisions regarding community affairs. What exactly does that look like? Maria's background as an administrator in the mayor's office has helped her learn to think critically about civic and political life. She has led countless community volunteer efforts—everything from bake sales to raise money for the local middle school to disaster relief efforts following a hurricane.

UNLEASHING CIVIC GIFTS

Our world needs everyone who has been entrusted with civic gifts, like Sara, to use their gifts for the good of as many people around them as possible. But as we've seen, civic gifts are not commonly noticed, put to use, or developed, so remember to appreciate and celebrate these gifts whenever you see them—whether in yourself or in others. This is one small way we can help unleash these less celebrated but highly important gifts.

Choose a specific person and vocation from the previous exercise and brainstorm ways the person could pursue growth in one or more of these three areas. (Remember to think about growth in knowledge, attitude, and skills.)

_____
has civic gifts.

Area to use their gift:
(circle one)

🏠 Family   ✝ Church

💼 Work   🌐 Society

Brainstorm ways
to pursue growth:

Intercultural Gifts

> *He made from one man every nation of*
> *mankind to live on all the face of the earth.*
>
> **ACTS 17:26**

> *Understand the differences; act on the commonalities.*
>
> **ANDREW MASONDO,**
> **SOUTH AFRICAN MATHEMATICIAN**

I n our work together at Lutheran Hour Ministries, we have the honor of working with a team of regional directors who help oversee and support our ministry centers in over thirty countries across the globe.

The joys and complexities of working across such a wide variety of cultures make intercultural gifts a must-have for our regional directors. Their language skills, respect for others, and ability to understand cultural differences are impressive to behold and allow our global work to thrive not only in North America but also in Africa, the Middle East, Asia, Europe, and Latin America.

You don't have to regularly travel to several different countries as our regional directors do to have or need intercultural gifts. In our increasingly diverse society, these gifts are tremendously important. Whether you use these gifts on the job, at home, in the neighborhood, or in public spaces, *intercultural gifts help you relate to people from other cultures and social groups.*

While many people have intercultural gifts, there are some people, like our regional directors, for whom these gifts are a bigger part of life. In a national survey, 7 percent of respondents listed the intercultural gift as their primary gift, and another 7 percent listed it as their secondary gift.

DISCOVERING INTERCULTURAL GIFTS

We are going to explore what it looks like to share intercultural gifts in different areas of life and what it looks like to grow these gifts over time, but first consider who in your life (including yourself!) may have intercultural gifts.

List people you know who may have intercultural gifts.

Intercultural gifts *help you relate to people from other cultures and social groups. Gifts include language skills, respect for others, and the ability to understand cultural differences.*

SHARING INTERCULTURAL GIFTS

Intercultural gifts aren't just helpful when you travel to another country. Life is filled with moments when you get to relate to people from other cultures and social groups. In those moments, it is so helpful when those with intercultural gifts don't assume that everyone can navigate those moments with the same grace they naturally can. Instead, what a blessing it is when they share their gifts—no matter where these moments take place.

To get a picture of what this could look like, let's consider the relevance of intercultural gifts to four different vocations in life. For each area we will also consider the case study of Isabel. No matter where Isabel goes, it seems that she has ample opportunities to share her intercultural gifts.

Family: Cultural diversity within families is on the rise. Modern households are becoming an intersection of various generations, ethnicities, religious perspectives, and even socioeconomic levels. The ability to navigate and translate between the variety of cultures within a household is vital to household health.

When Isabel's oldest son, Fred, ran into unexpected frustrations and miscommunications with his new girlfriend, Isabel's intercultural gifts came in handy. She helped Fred understand how his urban background and his girlfriend's rural background constituted a cultural difference that they could learn to navigate with curiosity and grace.

Church: The church as the body of Christ is composed of people from every nation, tribe, people, and language (Revelation 7:9). The cultural diversity of the church is more than demographic description, it is divine design. Embracing this diversity as a gift of God by working interculturally strengthens both the church's ministry and witness.

Isabel's church has a long-held tradition of hosting international church leaders. At times, though, language differences create barriers between the congregation and the leaders they are hosting. Isabel's language skills have allowed her to grease the social wheels and create meaningful connections during these important visits.

Work: Cultural diversity in the workplace creates opportunities and insights not always found in a more monocultural workplace. Businesses have discovered the power of diversity to create more productive and creative teams. The gift of intercultural communication is becoming one of the most important gifts one can bring to their workplace.

Isabel loves her administrative position in the international student office at the local university. Her respect for others and ability to understand cultural differences make her whole team more successful in their work with international students.

Society: While people who live in the same area may share some cultural characteristics, cultural diversity is always present in one form or another. Healthy societies seek to be inclusive of the various cultures within them that are striving for a sense of belonging and social cohesion.

The neighborhood association meetings for Isabel's diverse neighborhood can be fun, food-filled events. But at times, these meetings can be punctuated with misunderstandings. Isabel's ability to help sort out misunderstandings have allowed the fun of the meetings to win out over the brief moments of frustration.

Brainstorm ways to share intercultural gifts in each of these four areas. (Keep in mind the people you listed in the previous exercise.)

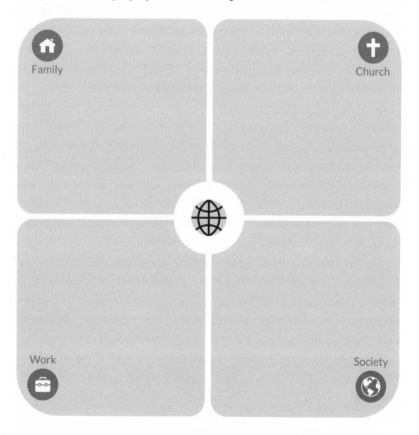

GROWING INTERCULTURAL GIFTS

Only 17 percent of those with intercultural gifts test as having achieved exemplary mastery of them, while 20 percent test as accomplished, and 63 percent are in the developing range.

63%	20%	17%
DEVELOPING	ACCOMPLISHED	EXEMPLARY

For those who want to grow their intercultural gifts, there are three basic areas in which to pursue growth.

Language skills involve listening, speaking, reading, and writing a language with proficiency. What does this look like in practice? Dr. Nimura has a gift for acquiring new languages. Born and raised in Japan, he studied English as a second language in high school and college. He enjoys learning the phonetics, intonations, and meanings of a new language. Dr. Nimura loves immersing himself in other cultures while studying—he believes this allows him to learn a new language quickly and authentically.

Respect for others involves honoring people for who they are with regard to their culture and background. Peter finds himself being drawn to those in his community who come from other cultures. One of his favorite weekend activities is hosting dinner parties with internationals and hearing their stories. Everyone in Peter's life knows that he deeply enjoys learning about and caring for others.

Ability to understand cultural differences involves discerning the various characteristics of a specific culture that differ from one's own. Leah's worldview was shaped by the years she spent overseas during high school. Leah sees cultural differences as making people vibrant, unique human beings. She loves to travel to different cultures, immersing herself as much as possible to learn about the beautiful differences in the ways people understand and interact with the world.

UNLEASHING INTERCULTURAL GIFTS

In our increasingly diverse and globally connected society, intercultural gifts are becoming even more important and vital all the time. We need everyone who has been entrusted with intercultural gifts, like Lutheran Hour Ministries' regional directors, to use their gifts for the good of as many people around them as possible. Be sure to appreciate and celebrate intercultural gifts whenever you see them—whether in yourself or in others. This is one small way we can help unleash these important gifts.

Choose a specific person and vocation from the previous exercise and brainstorm ways the person could pursue growth in one or more of these three areas. (Remember to think about growth in knowledge, attitude, and skills.)

_____
has intercultural gifts.

Area to use their gift:
(circle one)

Family   Church

Work   Society

Brainstorm ways
to pursue growth:

Communication Gifts

So also the tongue is a small member,
yet it boasts of great things.

JAMES 3:5

If you just communicate, you can get by.
But if you communicate skillfully,
you can work miracles.

JIM ROHN, AMERICAN ENTREPRENEUR

During his freshman year of high school, Don was approached by an English teacher who thought he should consider getting involved in the school's speech and debate team. Don didn't even know there was such a team, but this teacher (who also happened to coach the team) told Don that she could tell he had an aptitude and some innate abilities that would make him a natural.

Don did try out for the team, and for the next four years of high school he learned a wide variety of skills that helped him grow and mature as a communicator. From organizing thoughts to using compelling sources, from speaking with clear diction to using purposeful body language, from thinking on his feet to reading an audience, Don acquired a variety of rhetorical skills that helped him sharpen his communication gifts.

You don't have to be giving a formal speech or debating someone to use communication gifts, of course. Everyday life is filled with communication. We all communicate our way through life. Whether innate or learned, *all communication gifts help you communicate with individuals or groups in a clear and engaging way.*

While we all have some communication gifts we were either born with or picked up along the way, there are some people for whom these gifts are a bigger part of their lives. In a national survey, 11 percent of respondents listed the communication gift as their primary gift and another 9 percent listed it as their secondary gift.

DISCOVERING COMMUNICATION GIFTS

We are going to examine what it looks like to share communication gifts in different areas of life and what it looks like to grow these gifts over time, but first consider who in your life (including yourself!) may have communication gifts.

List people you know who may have communication gifts.

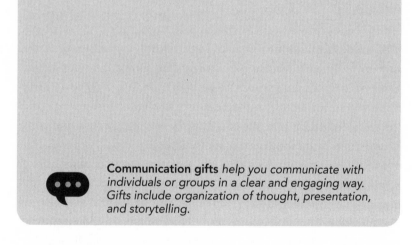

Communication gifts *help you communicate with individuals or groups in a clear and engaging way. Gifts include organization of thought, presentation, and storytelling.*

SHARING COMMUNICATION GIFTS

While we all communicate in one way or another as we go through our days, it's another thing entirely for someone with communication gifts to purposefully look to share those gifts in their different vocations.

To get a picture of what that could look like, let's consider the relevance of communication gifts in four different areas of life. For each area we will also consider the case study of Corey. From the time he learned to talk, Corey has been called golden-tongued by his family. Thankfully Corey decided early on in life to be generous with his God-given communication gifts.

Family: Clear communication in the household is at the core of building and maintaining deep and meaningful relationships. If communication is frustrated, household ties can quickly begin to unravel. Using and developing communication gifts within both one's core and extended household is one of the easiest ways to increase family health and well-being.

Corey's extended family has a tradition of holding monthly family parties, and Corey's creative storytelling has become one of the highlights of these parties. When one of Corey's nieces or nephews begs "make us up a story!" everyone gathers to be regaled by another creative, joyful, funny story that Corey makes up on the spot.

Church: At the heart of the church is the communication of the gospel message—a message that needs to be conveyed clearly and faithfully. In fact, everything the church does is a form of gospel communication. From Scripture to worship services, the importance of using communication gifts is at the heart of Christian ministry and life.

As a liturgist at his home church, Corey regularly reads the week's Scripture texts from a lectern just prior to the sermon. Not only have Corey's clear, unhurried, feeling-infused readings brought people's attention to the texts in a heightened way, but the other liturgists have begun to ask Corey to coach them in their own presentation skills.

Work: If there is a place where you can never have enough communication, it's the workplace. Communication is vital in leading a group of talented people to work together to achieve an organization's mission. The gift of communication is highly valued in the workplace both for those who work within an organization and those the organization serves.

As a middle manager at a large tech company, Corey's ability to organize his thoughts and present them clearly is a huge relief to his direct reports, who previously felt unheard and out of the loop.

Society: Communication is one of the most powerful forces in our local communities. Those entrusted with channels of communication can either unite or divide a society. Free and trustworthy communication is a necessity for a stable and healthy society. Growing and sharing the gift of communication is key in today's information-based societies.

Corey is a member of the local school board, and on more than one occasion, he's been tapped to present a seemingly complex issue at a public meeting. Corey's ability to organize his thoughts and clearly present material has served the board's ability to bring clarity among the public around important issues.

Brainstorm ways to share communication gifts in each of these four areas. (Keep in mind the people you listed in the previous exercise.)

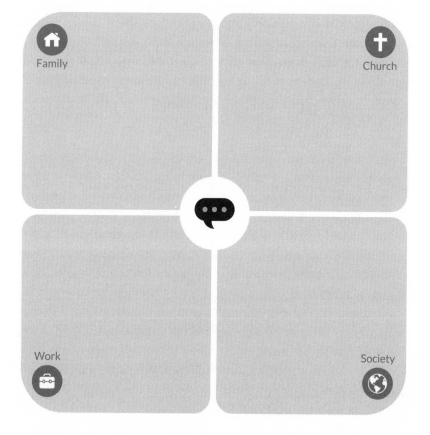

Family

Church

Work

Society

GROWING COMMUNICATION GIFTS

Nationally, only 9 percent of those with communication gifts test as having achieved exemplary mastery of them, while 26 percent test as accomplished, and 65 percent are in the developing range.

65%	26%	9%
DEVELOPING	ACCOMPLISHED	EXEMPLARY

For those who want to grow their communication gifts, there are three basic areas in which to pursue growth.

Organization of thought involves structuring information for smooth and cohesive presentation. What does this look like in practice? Alexandria is a newsroom editor who prides herself in knowing how to organize pieces of information in such a way that all the stories being presented by her company flow and intersect with one another in a smooth and cohesive manner for their audience.

Presentation involves sharing information and experiences in an engaging and dynamic manner. Christian is an author and narrator who travels the country to speak at schools. Christian's gift of presentation is made apparent in his stage presence. Christian knows how to keep his audience, both young and old, engaged as he shares information and experiences with them.

Storytelling involves sharing stories designed to uplift, guide, and interpret the world through the written and spoken word. Ever since she was a little girl, Lyra has loved to tell stories. Whether around the table with her family, at work with friends, or writing in her journal, Lyra interprets the world through stories and finds ways to uplift and guide others with the spoken word.

UNLEASHING COMMUNICATION GIFTS

James was right when he observed that the tongue "boasts of great things" (James 3:5). Our voices can be used to tear down or to build up, so we need people who've been entrusted with communication gifts to use their gifts for the good of as many people around them as possible. Rather than assume those with these gifts have discovered their gifts and are purposeful in how they share and grow them, let's appreciate and celebrate communication gifts whenever we see them—whether in ourselves or in others. This is one small way we can help unleash these important gifts.

Choose a specific person and vocation from the previous exercise and brainstorm ways the person could pursue growth in one or more of these three areas. (Remember to think about growth in knowledge, attitude, and skills.)

_____
has communication gifts.

Area to use their gift:
(circle one)

Family   Church

Work   Society

Brainstorm ways
to pursue growth:

Leadership Gifts

> *Where there is no guidance, a people falls,*
> *but in an abundance of counselors there is safety.*
>
> **PROVERBS 11:14**

> *You don't have to hold a position in order to be a leader.*
>
> **HENRY FORD, AMERICAN INDUSTRIALIST**

The two of us grew up hundreds of miles apart from each other, but our early years had this in common: we both grew up as reticent leaders.

We were content to work behind the scenes and not be the center of attention or source of leadership. Tony often said he'd rather be Alfred than Batman, and Don often said he wouldn't mind being left alone in a cabin in the woods. Yet we have found people following us in life, and we've both had others point out what they called our leadership gifts.

Coming to terms with the leadership gifts God has entrusted to us has meant asking, How do we use these gifts? And how do we grow as leaders in our ability to teach and mentor, or in our flexibility and risk taking and team building and time management?

Leadership gifts are varied and diverse, of course, including aptitudes, innate abilities, and acquired skills. But at their core, *leadership gifts help you organize people to reach a shared goal and effectively lead them toward that goal.*

This can happen in all sorts of areas in life: from household, to church, to work, to various teams and associations in the community. Exercising leadership doesn't always require having an explicit leadership role, but it does involve making use of the gifts you have. In a national survey, 8 percent of respondents listed the leadership gift as their primary gift and another 7 percent listed it as their secondary gift.

DISCOVERING LEADERSHIP GIFTS

To learn more about leadership gifts, we are going to look at sharing leadership gifts in different areas of life and growing these gifts over time. But before we do that, consider who in your life (including yourself!) may have leadership gifts.

List people you know who may have leadership gifts.

Leadership gifts *help you organize people to reach a shared goal and effectively lead them toward that goal. Gifts include the ability to teach and mentor, flexibility, risk taking, team building, and time management.*

SHARING LEADERSHIP GIFTS

The importance of leadership gifts is demonstrated by a recent survey that found there are more than fifteen thousand books on leadership in print and articles on leadership number in the thousands each year.[1] Obviously, leadership is pretty important.

But how do leadership gifts intersect with every area of life? Let's consider the relevance of these gifts in four different vocations in life and also consider the case study of Lucy. While Lucy, a stay-at-home mom, has no official leadership role in an organization, she has been gifted with considerable leadership gifts and generously uses them throughout her life.

Family: Leadership in the household takes many forms. Every characteristic that makes a household a home needs to be led in one way or another. Sometimes household leadership takes the form of leading conversations and debates, at other times it means taking on the tasks assigned to the role one fills in the household. Household leadership can ebb and flow with different members leading in different areas of household life.

In addition to her three teenagers, Lucy is helping raise her sister's three young sons while her sister is stationed overseas. This calling in life has tapped many of Lucy's leadership gifts: her ability to teach and mentor, her flexibility, her team-building skills, and especially her time management prowess.

Church: Church leadership comes in many forms, from professional ministry leadership to lay volunteering. Leadership gifts in the church are essential for ministry development and growth. Those who possess leadership gifts can be an excellent example of what it means to be an active member of a ministry, while at the same time providing the necessary leadership roles for moving ministry forward.

For years Lucy has led a team of hosts and ushers at her local church. She takes this responsibility seriously, regularly coaching members of her team in how to sharpen their hospitality and interactions. She also plans short team-building moments that keep her teammates excited to serve and focused on their important goals as a team.

Work: Few areas of society have explored the role of leadership more than the workplace, in part because without appropriate leadership most businesses fail. Countless books and courses exist to grow and unleash leadership gifts within businesses and organizations. There is always a place for leadership gifts at work.

When Lucy and her friends back in college started a small business, Lucy's flexibility and risk taking had been a key contribution to the company's leadership team. She was also able to initiate some important team building among the staff.

Society: Leadership gifts are to be shared in the community not to benefit the individual but to benefit the larger community and its residents. Leadership in the community is often informal and associational and, at times, can lack the funding and resources that larger civic efforts command. This is part of why it is important to unleash leadership gifts throughout the community.

Lucy's greatest leadership contribution as president of her apartment complex tenants' association has been to clarify and focus the goal of the association and run meetings in such a way that the goal is central to all their business. The once meandering association has a new level of energy and direction thanks to Lucy's leadership gifts.

Brainstorm ways to share leadership gifts in each of these four areas. (Keep in mind the people you listed in the previous exercise.)

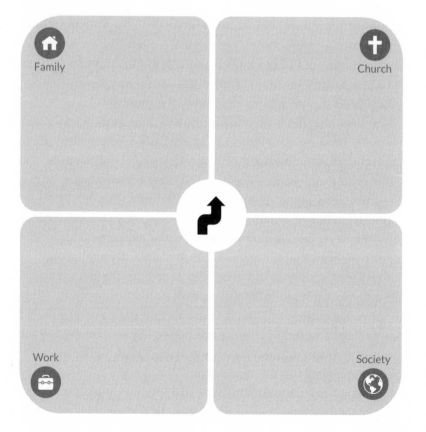

Family

Church

Work

Society

GROWING LEADERSHIP GIFTS

Only 19 percent of those with leadership gifts test as having achieved exemplary mastery, while 24 percent test as accomplished, and 57 percent are in the developing range.

57%	24%	19%
DEVELOPING	ACCOMPLISHED	EXEMPLARY

For those who want to grow their leadership gifts, there are five basic areas in which to pursue growth.

Teaching and mentoring involves sharing knowledge and experience through relational instruction and explanation. What does this look like in practice? Emmanuel works as a head nurse at a top-rated children's hospital. His role affords him the opportunity to teach and mentor department staff on a daily basis. Each time Emmanuel visits a patient or reports to the head physician, he brings other nurses with him so they can continue to learn more about how to effectively and safely tend to the children in their care.

Flexibility involves adapting to changing circumstances and expectations with agility and readiness. As a stay-at-home mom of three, Raisa models flexibility day in and day out. From managing the necessities of running a home to juggling school drop-offs and other kid-related responsibilities, Raisa takes pride in her ability to pivot on a dime and change plans while keeping the best interest of her family front and center.

Risk taking involves taking an action that involves uncertainty or possible loss in order to achieve a goal. A commercial diver by trade, Samir is used to taking risks on the job. Whether leading a team to examine submerged structures, repairing structural damage to an ocean liner, or setting explosives under water, Samir knows when risk taking is necessary and when to look for an alternative option.

Team building involves encouraging a group of people to work together to strengthen team roles and relationships. Kim is a children's choir director, and she genuinely loves working on team building with her young singers. From vocal warm-ups to encouraging students to assist each other with homework, Kim finds a way to turn each lesson into a fun and effective team-building exercise that will strengthen her students' trust in each other as well as themselves.

Time management involves exercising conscious control of time spent on specific activities to increase effectiveness and productivity. As a warehouse manager, Joseph uses his time management skills to plan out the most effective use of his hours on the job. Upon arriving at work each morning, he assesses what needs to get done that day, how long each task will take, and in what order each should be completed. Then he confidently sets out with his productive schedule mentally outlined.

UNLEASHING LEADERSHIP GIFTS

As we are reminded in Proverbs, without leadership "a people falls" (Proverbs 11:14). Leadership is integrally important to so much in life that it is crucial for as many leadership gifts to be unleashed as possible. So let's not take these gifts for granted; rather, let's appreciate and celebrate leadership gifts whenever we see them—whether in ourselves or in others. This is one small way we can help unleash these important gifts.

Choose a specific person and vocation from the previous exercise and brainstorm ways the person could pursue growth in one or more of these five areas. (Remember to think about growth in knowledge, attitude, and skills.)

_____ has leadership gifts.

Area to use their gift:
(circle one)

Family   Church

Work   Society

Brainstorm ways
to pursue growth:

Teamwork Gifts

> Though a man might prevail against
> one who is alone, two will withstand him—
> a threefold cord is not quickly broken.
> **ECCLESIASTES 4:12**

> Alone we can do so little, together we can do so much.
> **HELEN KELLER, AMERICAN AUTHOR AND ACTIVIST**

Have you ever been on a team with someone who seems to help everyone else on the team work together better? Sports coaches call these types "good locker room players." In one sense they function like glue (holding the team together), and in another they are like grease (helping all the pieces move smoothly with minimal friction).

These people have teamwork gifts. Their collaboration, communication, empathy, humility, positivity, and problem-solving go a long way in helping a team stay together and work well together.

Whether teamwork gifts are being used on a sports team, in a group at work, in a classroom, or in the household, *teamwork gifts help you effectively collaborate with and work alongside others.*

While all of us need to learn how to function well on teams, there are some people who, whether by aptitude, innate abilities, or acquired skills, have significant teamwork gifts. In a national survey, 10 percent of respondents listed teamwork gifts as their primary gift and another 12 percent listed it as their secondary gift.

DISCOVERING TEAMWORK GIFTS

To learn more about teamwork gifts we are going to examine what it looks like to share teamwork gifts in different areas of life and what it looks like to grow these gifts over time. But first, consider who in your life (including yourself!) may have teamwork gifts.

List people you know who may have teamwork gifts.

Teamwork gifts *help you effectively collaborate with and work alongside others. Gifts include collaboration, communication, empathy, humility, positivity, and problem-solving.*

SHARING TEAMWORK GIFTS

Teamwork isn't just relevant in the realm of sports. The reality is we function in teams in many areas of life—whether those teams are explicit (like a baseball team whose members are easily identifiable because of their uniforms) or more subtle (like a dozen people who happen to work the same shift at their job). This is why it's important for those with teamwork gifts to share those gifts in a wide variety of places.

Let's consider the relevance of teamwork gifts in four of life's callings. For each calling we will also consider the case study of Teresa.

Family: In many ways a household is the closest thing to a team found in society. All household members, with their specific roles and responsibilities, work together for the well-being of the whole household. Helping household members willingly participate in a positive way is one of the most important contributions that those with teamwork gifts can offer a household.

When Teresa's parents began to age, she and her four siblings were forced to navigate a tricky transition in life. Although her siblings all have big personalities and opinions, Teresa's positivity and ability to collaborate and problem-solve allowed her siblings to work together well as they helped their parents transition to a care facility.

Church: The church is, in one sense, a team of people with a variety of gifts working together to achieve the singular goal of gospel proclamation. Many congregations experience greater success in their mission when someone with teamwork gifts helps turn members' "I" and "me" to "we" and "us."

Teresa has often gone on the spring break mercy trip her church sends out each year. All the people who attend these projects become a team for a week—and a stressful week at that. Teresa's empathy and humility and communication allow her to draw people in and connect them with each other.

Work: Teamwork gifts within the workplace can transform an organization and enable it to achieve goals previously unattainable. The concept that "we are better together" is at the heart of working together in a diverse and inclusive team. When teamwork gifts are shared at work, individual contributions coalesce together and, many times, result in a product that is greater than the sum of its parts.

In her work at a midsized accounting firm, Teresa's team often has to work toward strict deadlines. When time gets short on a project, so do tempers, and this is when Teresa's positivity, problem-solving, and empathy come in handy. Her teamwork gifts allow her to ease tensions and increase communication.

Society: When teamwork gifts are used with a community, projects are achieved and the members' sense of ownership and inclusion increase. Considering that community property and projects are shared as a matter of definition, using teamwork gifts to include the greatest number of community members in managing and improving community resources is a natural and healthy approach.

Teresa is not the organizer of the volunteer mentoring program at the nearby elementary school, but many people see her as the "glue" that helps hold together the loose group of diverse volunteers. Teresa seems to know every volunteer mentor, and her empathy, humility, and positivity are part of what helps the afternoon mentoring program go so well.

Brainstorm ways to share teamwork gifts in each of these four areas. (Keep in mind the people you listed in the previous exercise.)

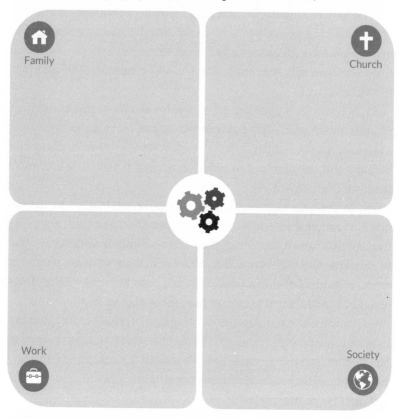

GROWING TEAMWORK GIFTS

Nationally, only 15 percent of those with teamwork gifts test as having achieved exemplary mastery of them, while 23 percent test as accomplished, and 62 percent are in the developing range.

62%	23%	15%
DEVELOPING	ACCOMPLISHED	EXEMPLARY

For those who want to grow their teamwork gifts, there are six basic areas in which to pursue growth.

Collaboration involves combining the gifts and ideas of multiple people to collectively achieve a goal. What does this look like in practice? As a college student, Matt spends his summers as a camp counselor. He loves collaborating with the other leaders to plan activities for the kids— something that requires creativity and trust in other team members.

Communication involves sending and receiving messages through verbal and nonverbal means in order to convey a clear meaning. Akeno is talented at explaining things to others in a clear and thoughtful way. He often relies on body language to emphasize the message he's trying to get across. Akeno is a good communicator and can effortlessly get everyone on the same page.

Empathy involves identifying with the feelings, thoughts, and experiences of another person. What exactly does that look like? Miriam is a school counselor whose empathy is used almost daily. An active and nonjudgmental listener, she is beloved by others and encourages those around her to practice empathy as well, by listening, acknowledging, learning, and acting in the best interest of others.

Humility involves appreciating the strengths of others without letting personal ego get in the way. Zahara is a youth worker who absolutely loves the teens she serves. While receiving a great deal of added attention from the younger crowd, Zahara does her best to lead with humility, remaining open to correction and learning new things. She hopes to be a good role model to others in her congregation.

Positivity involves being optimistic in attitude toward people and outcomes. What does this look like in practice? Lane, a high schooler whose positivity is infectious, is often described as cheerful, bubbly, bright, and energetic. Despite the dreariness of high school, the weighty responsibilities and goals put on her by adults, and the sometimes not-so-great days, Lane chooses to see the best in everyone and everything as she makes her mark on the world.

Problem-solving involves investigating a problem to determine its source and an effective solution. As a manager at a tech company,

Sharon is constantly problem-solving alongside her teammates as they tweak code and redesign facets of digital products. She is energized by these daily tasks; in her opinion, there is no greater feeling than pushing through a problem to the discovery of a solution.

UNLEASHING TEAMWORK GIFTS

As we are reminded in Ecclesiastes 4:12, "A threefold cord is not quickly broken." We are all stronger when we work together. This is why our world needs everyone who has been entrusted with teamwork gifts to unleash them for the good of those around them. Remember to appreciate and celebrate teamwork gifts whenever you see them—whether in yourself or in others. This is one small way we can help unleash these important gifts.

Choose a specific person and vocation from the previous exercise and brainstorm ways the person could pursue growth in one or more of these six areas. (Remember to think about growth in knowledge, attitude, and skills.)

The Importance of Every Gift

Whether you focused on just those gifts you believe God has entrusted to you or worked your way through all twelve gifts, we are so encouraged that you have invested time thinking about gifts. For even more resources on discovering, sharing, and growing gifts, visit www.lhm.org/gifted.

The reality is, we need all our gifts to be unleashed. We need your gifts, and you need ours and everyone else's. As Paul put it, we all have "gifts that differ" (Romans 12:6). This is God's way: to entrust different gifts to each of us so that we must partner together to do all of the good, flourishing work he's planned for us. We are created to be blessed by others' gifts as much as we're created to bless others with our own gifts.

And that's part of what makes this process of discovering, sharing, and growing our gifts so important and vital and exciting. God entrusted us with gifts so that we would use them. He gave us gifts that differ and, as a result, we are called to both give and receive these gifts.

"Having gifts that differ according to the grace given to us, let us use them" (Romans 12:6).

May we do just that: may we use not some of our gifts or only a few people's gifts . . . but every gift God has given to every one of us.

Notes

INTRODUCTION

[1]Gene Edward Veith, *Working for Our Neighbor* (Grand Rapids, MI: Christian's Library Press, 2016), xv.

[2]Paul D. Stanley and J. Robert Clinton, *Connecting: The Mentoring Relationships You Need to Succeed in Life* (Colorado Springs, CO: NavPress, 1992), 222.

[3]Barna Group, *Gifted for More: A Framework for Equipping Christians to Share Their Abilities and Skills in Everyday Life* (Ventura, CA: Barna, 2021).

[4]Don Everts, *Discover Your Gifts: Celebrating How God Made You and Everyone You Know* (Downers Grove, IL: InterVarsity Press, 2021).

1 TECHNICAL GIFTS

[1]Barna Group, September 3–12, 2020, quantitative survey.

[2]Lutheran Hour Ministries and Barna developed eight markers of mastery in light of current research on skill development. Individuals with seven or eight of the markers were categorized as exemplary; those with four to six of the markers were categorized as accomplished; and those with three or fewer markers were categorized as developing. You can learn more about the marks of mastery on pages 70-77 of Barna Group, *Gifted for More: A Framework for Equipping Christians to Share Their Abilities and Skills in Everyday Life* (Ventura, CA: Barna, 2021).

11 LEADERSHIP GIFTS

[1]Michael Shinagel, "The Paradox of Leadership," *Harvard Division of Continuing Education: Professional Development* (blog), July 3, 2013, https://professional. dce.harvard.edu/blog/the-paradox-of-leadership.

THE HOPEFUL NEIGHBORHOOD PROJECT ®

The Hopeful Neighborhood Project is a collaborative network committed to improving neighborhood well-being around the world. Our resources and online network equip and encourage neighbors to work together, using their gifts and the gifts of their community, to pursue the common good of their neighborhood.

*To find out more about our
active network and many resources visit us at
hopefulneighborhood.org.*

Also Available

Discover Your Gifts
978-1-5140-0373-2